Tuli Rose

Clocks Tick Like Marshmallows

Peek Inside

The Unseen Cost of 'Later'

In a world that celebrates the 'hustle', procrastination is often painted as the villain — sneaky, unproductive, and universally unwanted. Yet, here we stand, not to vilify it, but to understand its allure and the lessons hidden within its grasp. This book, is an odyssey into the heart of our delays, a whimsical yet profound journey to discover the silver linings in postponed decisions, and ultimately, a guide to harnessing the power of 'later' for financial gain.

We've all been there — the moment when deciding between the immediate pleasure of 'now' and the distant benefits of 'later' feels like an internal tug of war. It's not just about being lazy or disorganized; it's about human nature's complex dance with time, gratification, and the unexpected softness of moments that stretch and expand, much like marshmallows, allowing for a deeper reflection and a richer experience.

Our first stop in this exploration? Understanding why we procrastinate, especially when our financial future is at stake. The title of our journey, "Clocks Tick Like Marshmallows," serves as a gentle reminder that time, with its perceived rigidity and relentless march forward, can also be soft, malleable, and surprisingly sweet, offering us a unique perspective on how we view our moments of delay.

But fear not. This is not a sermon from the mountaintop. Instead, it's a conversation between fellow travelers who've stumbled, delayed, and, yes, procrastinated, only to realize that within every moment of delay, there's potential for insight, growth, and strategic planning. The marshmallow-like quality of time invites us to savor the process, to immerse ourselves in the richness of contemplation, and to discover the myriad ways in which procrastination can be a gateway to creativity and innovation.

As we delve into the psychology of procrastination, we'll uncover not just the roots of this habit but also the fruits it can bear when approached with curiosity and intention. Together, we'll transform procrastination from a source of guilt into a tool for financial empowerment, learning to make time our ally in the quest for prosperity. We'll explore how the soft, stretching moments — those marshmallow-like pauses — can become fertile ground for seeding future successes.

Welcome to a journey of financial enlightenment, where 'later' becomes not just a time, but a place brimming with potential. Let's embrace the journey, one thoughtful delay at a time, and discover how the seemingly incongruous elements of clocks and marshmallows can coalesce into a powerful philosophy for life and investing.

The Procrastination Plague

The Siren Call of Tomorrow

It begins with a whisper, a gentle nudge towards the comfort of "later." "There's always tomorrow," it coos, wrapping its seductive tendrils around our intentions. This is the voice of procrastination, a master of disguise, cloaked in the guise of benign delay. Yet, beneath its soothing promises lies a thief, robbing us of time, opportunity, and, most critically, our financial well-being.

Understanding the Beast

To conquer procrastination, we must first understand it. It's not born from laziness or a lack of ambition. No, it's far more complex. It stems from a cocktail of fear — fear of failure, fear of the unknown, and, paradoxically, fear of success. It's fueled by the overwhelming nature of our tasks and a deep-seated preference for instant gratification. Our brains are wired to seek immediate rewards, making the deferred gratification of financial planning and saving seem less appealing.

The Financial Fallout

The impact of procrastination on our finances can be devastating. It's the unchecked subscriptions that drain our accounts, the late fees that pile up unnoticed, and the investments never made that could have compounded into financial freedom. Each decision postponed is a step not taken towards our financial goals, a brick laid on the path to potential fiscal stress.

A Practical Approach to Combat

- **Acknowledge the Habit:** The first step is admitting that procrastination has taken hold of your financial decisions.

Recognize the patterns and triggers that lead you to delay important financial tasks.

- **Break It Down:** Large financial goals can seem daunting. Break them into smaller, manageable tasks. Instead of "save for retirement," start with "open a retirement account" or "set up a monthly transfer to savings."

- **Set Clear, Achievable Goals:** Specificity is your ally. Instead of vaguely aiming to "invest more," set a goal to "invest $100 in a low-cost index fund every month."

- **Embrace Automation:** Use technology to your advantage. Automate your savings, bill payments, and investments. If you don't see the money, you're less likely to miss it.

- **Celebrate Small Wins:** Each step towards your financial goal is progress. Celebrate these moments to build momentum and reinforce positive behavior.

- **Seek Accountability:** Share your financial goals with a trusted friend or family member. Regular check-ins can provide the external push needed to stay on track.

- **Educate Yourself:** Knowledge is power. Understanding the basics of personal finance can demystify the process, making it less intimidating to take the first step.

The procrastination plague, while pervasive, is not invincible. With awareness, a plan of attack, and a sprinkle of discipline, we can reclaim our financial future from its grasp. Remember, the best time to start was yesterday. The next best time? Today. Let's turn the page on procrastination and script a new chapter in our financial journey — one marked by action, progress, and prosperity.

By understanding procrastination's roots and implementing practical strategies, we can overcome this hurdle, making way for a healthier financial life. This chapter serves as the foundation for a transformative journey from procrastination to action, setting the stage for the comprehensive strategies and insights to come.

The Psychology Behind the Procrastination

Unraveling the Procrastination Puzzle

Procrastination isn't just a barrier to completing tasks; it's a complex psychological puzzle that affects our financial decisions and behaviors. Understanding the psychological underpinnings of procrastination can arm us with the tools needed to combat it effectively. It's time to delve into the mental mechanics that fuel procrastination and outline practical strategies to navigate and overcome these challenges.

The Fear Factor

At the heart of procrastination lies fear. Fear of making the wrong decision, fear of loss, and even fear of success can paralyze us, keeping our finances in a stagnant state.

Practical Strategy: Normalize Fear

- **Acknowledge Your Fears:** Write them down. Seeing fears on paper can diminish their power.

- **Educate Yourself:** Financial fears often stem from a lack of understanding. Use resources to learn about financial products and investment strategies to demystify them.

- **Start Small:** Begin with low-risk financial decisions to build confidence.

Overwhelm and Decision Fatigue
The vast array of financial choices can lead to decision fatigue, making it easier to postpone decisions than to make them.

Practical Strategy: Simplify Choices

- **Limit Options:** When saving or investing, start with a few clear options. Analysis paralysis can be mitigated by narrowing down choices.

- **Use Financial Tools:** Apps and online calculators can simplify decision-making processes by providing personalized recommendations based on your goals and risk tolerance.

Instant Gratification vs. Long-Term Rewards

Our brains are wired to prioritize immediate rewards over future benefits, a trait that directly conflicts with effective financial planning.

Practical Strategy: Visualize the Future

- **Create a Vision Board:** Visual reminders of your financial goals can help align your present actions with your future benefits.

- **Implement a Reward System:** Reward yourself for meeting small financial milestones. This can help bridge the gap between immediate and delayed gratification.

Self-Doubt and Perfectionism

The quest for the perfect financial plan can lead to procrastination. The fear of making an imperfect choice can halt progress.

Practical Strategy: Embrace Imperfection

- **Set 'Good Enough' Goals:** Aim for progress, not perfection. A good financial plan that you adhere to is better than a perfect one that never materializes.

- **Learn from Mistakes:** View financial setbacks as learning opportunities, not failures. Each mistake is a step towards mastering your finances.

The Role of Habit

Procrastination can become a deeply ingrained habit, making it challenging to break the cycle and take action.

Practical Strategy: Build New Habits

- **Start with Micro-Habits:** Incorporate small financial habits into your daily routine. Even something as simple as checking your bank account daily can have a cumulative effect.

- **Use Habit Stacking:** Attach a new financial habit to an existing routine. For example, review your budget after your morning coffee.

The psychology behind procrastination is complex, but not insurmountable. By understanding the fears, overwhelming choices, and instant gratification desires that fuel our procrastination, we can tailor strategies to overcome these hurdles. Financial wellness begins with mental clarity and the courage to take the first step, however small, towards our goals. Let's transform our understanding into action, paving the way for a financially proactive future.

This chapter has demystified the psychological barriers to financial action, providing a roadmap to navigate and dismantle the procrastination that hinders our financial progress. With these insights and strategies, we're better equipped to face financial decisions with confidence, moving from inertia to action.

The Cost of "I'll Do It Later"

Time's Silent Toll on Wealth

Every moment spent in the grip of procrastination isn't just time lost; it's potential wealth that evaporates like morning mist under the sun. The true cost of "I'll do it later" extends far beyond missed deadlines and rushed decisions — it's the compound interest never earned, the investment opportunities missed, and the financial growth stunted. This chapter aims to illuminate the stark realities of financial procrastination and equip you with actionable strategies to reclaim control over your financial destiny.

The Compound Interest Opportunity Lost

One of the most compelling reasons to act now rather than later lies in the magic of compound interest. Albert Einstein reportedly called compound interest the eighth wonder of the world, for it can turn modest savings into a substantial nest egg over time.

Practical Strategy: Start Compounding Now

- **Automate Your Savings:** Set up automatic transfers to a savings or investment account. Even a small monthly amount can grow significantly over time.

- **Use a Compound Interest Calculator:** Visualize your potential gains by using online calculators. Seeing the numbers can be a powerful motivator to start saving now.

The High Price of Late Fees and Interest

Procrastination in paying bills or managing debt can lead to unnecessary late fees and higher interest payments

— money that could have been better spent or saved.

Practical Strategy: Automate and Negotiate

- **Automate Bill Payments:** Utilize your bank's auto-pay feature to ensure bills are paid on time, avoiding late fees.

- **Negotiate Interest Rates:** If you carry a balance on credit cards, call your creditors to negotiate a lower interest rate. Every percentage point reduced is money saved.

Missed Investment Opportunities
In the world of investing, timing can be everything. Procrastinating on investment decisions can mean missing out on market upswings or buying in at a peak rather than a trough.

Practical Strategy: Embrace Dollar-Cost Averaging

- **Start with Regular, Small Investments:** Investing a fixed amount regularly reduces the risk of trying to time the market and mitigates the impact of volatility.

- **Stay Informed, But Don't Obsess:** Keep abreast of market trends without becoming paralyzed by the fear of making the wrong decision.

The Emotional Cost

Beyond the tangible financial costs, procrastination exacts a heavy emotional toll, leading to stress, anxiety, and a sense of being overwhelmed — emotions that can further impede our ability to make sound financial decisions.

Practical Strategy: Cultivate Financial Mindfulness

- **Set Aside Time for Financial Planning:** Dedicate a regular, uninterrupted time each week to manage your finances. This can reduce the stress of feeling unprepared.

- **Practice Gratitude:** Focusing on what you have, rather than what you lack, can shift your perspective and reduce the anxiety associated with financial decisions.

The cost of procrastination is not just measured in dollars and cents but in the peace of mind forfeited and the opportunities lost. Recognizing and confronting the real price of delaying financial decisions can be the catalyst we need to start taking immediate action. By implementing practical, proactive strategies to manage our finances, we not only safeguard our wealth but also invest in our overall well-being and future prosperity.

Armed with the knowledge of the true cost of procrastination and practical tools to combat it, we can begin to forge a path toward financial security and freedom. Let this chapter serve as a turning point, inspiring you to act now for a richer tomorrow.

Slaying the Procrastination Dragon

The Battle Begins

Embarking on a quest to slay the dragon of procrastination requires more than mere desire; it demands a strategic plan, a shield of determination, and the sword of action. This chapter is your war room, where strategies are formulated, weapons are forged, and the battle plan against financial procrastination is drawn. The dragon's fire breathes excuses and delays, but armed with the right approach, its flames can be extinguished, leading to a kingdom of financial prosperity and growth.

Forge Your Weapons: Time Management Meets Financial Planning

The first step in our battle is to forge two critical weapons: the Shield of

Time Management and the Sword of Financial Planning. Together, they form an invincible arsenal against procrastination.

Practical Strategy: Equip Yourself

- **Time Blocking for Financial Tasks:** Dedicate specific blocks of time in your calendar for managing finances. Treat these blocks as non-negotiable appointments with your future self.

- **The "Two-Minute Rule" for Immediate Action:** If a financial task can be done in two minutes or less, do it immediately. This rule helps in tackling small tasks before they pile up into a daunting backlog.

Understanding the Enemy: Breaking Down Financial Tasks

Procrastination thrives on the vague and undefined. By breaking down financial goals into specific, actionable tasks, the dragon's power wanes, and its intimidation factor diminishes.

Practical Strategy: Dissect the Beast

- **SMART Goals for Finances:** Define your financial goals as Specific, Measurable, Achievable, Relevant, and Time-bound. This clarity transforms overwhelming objectives into manageable quests.

- **Task Decomposition:** Break down each financial goal into smaller tasks. Instead of "Save for retirement," list tasks like "Research retirement accounts," "Decide on a monthly saving amount," and "Set up automatic transfer to retirement fund."

Facing the Fire: Overcoming Fear and Resistance

The dragon's fiercest weapon is the fire of fear and resistance that it breathes, paralyzing would-be financial warriors. Facing this fire head-on is a pivotal step in the battle.

Practical Strategy: Don the Armor of Knowledge

- **Educational Shields:** Arm yourself with knowledge by reading books, attending workshops, or using online resources to understand financial concepts, reducing fear through understanding.

- **Mindfulness Meditation:** Practice mindfulness to calm the mind and reduce anxiety related to financial decisions. This mental clarity can extinguish the flames of fear.

The Charge: Taking Action

With weapons forged and strategies laid, the time comes to charge into battle. Taking action, despite the dragon's intimidating presence, is the ultimate act of courage in our quest.

Practical Strategy: Small Steps, Big Leaps

- **Incremental Progress:** Embrace the power of small, consistent actions. Even tiny steps forward accumulate into significant progress over time.

- **Celebrate Victories:** Acknowledge and celebrate each victory, no matter how small, to build momentum and confidence.

Slaying the procrastination dragon is not a tale of overnight heroism but a saga of persistence, strategy, and gradual triumphs. As you apply these practical approaches to your financial life, you'll find the dragon's formidable facade beginning to crumble, revealing the path to a prosperous and financially secure kingdom that was yours to claim all along.

By the end of this chapter, you are no longer a bystander in your financial story but a valiant warrior, equipped and ready to conquer procrastination and usher in an era of financial empowerment and growth. Let the battle cry sound, for the dragon awaits, and victory is within reach.

The Procrastinator's Guide to Investing

So, You Think Investing is for Tycoons and Geniuses? Think Again.

Welcome to the club — the "I'll think about investing tomorrow" club. The club's favorite activities include staring blankly at stock market news, making vague plans to "get into investing" one day, and spending that would-be investment money on things we don't need. Sound familiar? Buckle up, because we're about to turn that ship around.

Investing: Not Just for the Suits

First off, let's debunk the myth that investing is a high-falutin' activity reserved for people who use words like "portfolio" in casual conversation. Investing is for everyone. Yes, even for us, the champions of "I'll do it later."

Practical Strategy: Start Simple and Speak Human

- **Acronym Soup is Off the Menu:** ETFs, IRAs, and all those other fancy acronyms? They're just fancy ways to say "ways to make your money work for you." Let's keep it that way.

- **The One-Fund Wonder:** Start with something straightforward, like an index fund or a target-date fund. Think of it as the crockpot of investing—you set it, forget it, and let it cook up some returns over time.

The "Five-Minute-or-Less" Investment Plan

Who says you need to devote hours to start investing? Not us. Here's how you can get started in less time than it takes to choose a Netflix show.

Practical Strategy: Quick-Start Investing

- **Download an Investment App:** Pick one, any one. Seriously, most are user-friendly and designed for us procrastinators.

- **Sign Up, Look Around:** Take a quick tour. No need to commit to anything yet. Just dip your toes.

- **Set a Reminder:** Put a reminder in your phone for later (because, you know, procrastination) to revisit and maybe invest a little.

Fear of Losing Money: The Ultimate Procrastination Excuse

Let's address the elephant in the room. The fear of losing money can freeze us in our tracks. Here's the kicker: doing nothing is also a risk. Inflation is like a silent account-drainer, slowly but surely reducing your money's purchasing power.

Practical Strategy: Embrace the Turtle, Not the Hare

- **Start with Risk-Free Investments:** Consider starting with a high-yield savings account or certificates of deposit (CDs). They're the financial equivalent of a weighted blanket — comforting and low risk.

- **Dabble with Dollar-Cost Averaging:** Invest a small, fixed amount regularly. It's like dipping your toes in the pool instead of cannonballing into the deep end.

But What About All Those Investment Choices?

Choice overload is real. But here's a secret: you don't have to choose everything. You're not at a buffet.

Practical Strategy: Keep It Lean

- **Focus on One or Two Investments:** Seriously, you don't need a smorgasbord. Start with one index fund, then get fancy later if you feel like it.

- **Ignore the Noise:** Everyone has an opinion. Aunt Edna thinks gold is the way to go; your buddy swears by Bitcoin. Nod politely, then do your own thing.

Investing doesn't require a suit, a degree in finance, or a crystal ball. It just requires you to start — somewhere, anywhere. Let this be the nudge you need to move from "I'll think about investing tomorrow" to "I did a thing today." And remember, in the world of investing, being a tortoise is totally fine. Slow and steady wins the race, after all.

By embracing these down-to-earth strategies, you're not just dipping your toes into the world of investing; you're taking a proactive step towards securing your financial future. And who knows? Maybe one day, you'll be the one casually dropping "portfolio" into conversations — not because you have to, but because you want to.

Your Financial Action Plan

You've made it through the procrastination jungle and the investing maze, probably with a few eye rolls and some chuckles along the way. Now, you're standing at the edge of the "Actually Doing Things" cliff. Scary? Maybe a little. Exciting? Absolutely. It's time to roll up those sleeves (or don't, if you're wearing a tank top) and craft a financial action plan that even the most dedicated procrastinator can stick to.

Step 1: The 'Not-So-Secret' Financial Vision Board

Yeah, yeah, vision boards might sound like something straight out of a self-help guru's handbook, but stick with us here. Having a clear picture of what you want your financial life to look like can be surprisingly motivating.

Practical Strategy: Get Crafty (or Digital)

- **Cut and Paste or Click and Drag:** Whether you're more scissors-and-glue or drag-and-drop, make a collage of your financial goals. Dream house? Early retirement? That trip to Japan? Get it all on there.

- **Location, Location, Location:** Put your vision board somewhere you'll see it every day. Fridge door, bathroom mirror, or as your phone's wallpaper — somewhere you can't ignore it.

Step 2: The 'Breaking It Down' Boogie
Big goals are great, but they can also feel like trying to eat a whale in one bite. Not recommended.

Practical Strategy: Slice and Dice

- **Monthly Milestones:** Break down your big goals into monthly or even weekly milestones. Want to save $1,200 in a year? That's $100 a month or $25 a week. Suddenly, that whale's looking a lot more digestible.

- **The Checklist Charm:** There's something deeply satisfying about crossing things off a list. Make a checklist of your milestones and enjoy that sweet, sweet dopamine hit every time you tick one off.

Step 3: The 'Automate to Accumulate' Shuffle

Remember how we talked about setting your savings and investments on auto-pilot? Here's where that gets real.

Practical Strategy: Set and Forget (But Check In Occasionally)

- **Direct Deposit Diversion:** Have a portion of your paycheck automatically diverted into a savings or investment account. You can't spend what you don't see.

- **Bill Pay, the Automatic Way:** Automate those bill payments to avoid late fees and the procrastination tax.

Step 4: The 'Knowledge is Power, But Don't Go Overboard' Waltz

Staying informed is great, but there's a fine line between being knowledgeable and falling down a financial advice rabbit hole.

Practical Strategy: Curate Your Consumption

- **Pick Your Poison:** Find one or two financial news sources or blogs that resonate with you. You don't need to follow every finance guru on social media.

- **Timely Tutorials:** Dedicate a small, specific chunk of time each week to learning something new about finances. Keep it brief to avoid overwhelm.

Step 5: The 'Accounta-Buddy' Boogie

Going solo on your financial journey can be tough. Why not recruit a friend to boogie through the budgeting and saving saga with you?

Practical Strategy: Team Up for Success

- **Find a Financial Friend:** Pair up with someone who shares similar financial goals. Check in with each other weekly to share successes, setbacks, and tips.

- **Celebrate Together:** Hit a milestone? Celebrate together. Having an accounta-buddy turns financial management from a chore into a shared adventure.

Creating a financial action plan doesn't have to be a drag. By tackling it with creativity, breaking it down into bite-sized pieces, automating the boring bits, staying just informed enough, and bringing a friend along for the ride, you can turn financial planning from a dreaded task into a fun, rewarding part of your life. Remember, the goal isn't to be perfect; it's to be better than yesterday. So, let's do this thing — one boogie step at a time.

And just like that, you're not just planning; you're doing. You're taking control of your financial future with a practical action plan that even the most notorious procrastinators can follow. "Actually Doing Things" club; the view from here is pretty great.

Automate to Accumulate

The "Set It and Forget It" Financial Feast

Alright, let's talk turkey. And by turkey, I mean the juicy, can't-miss opportunity to make your money work for you while you sleep, binge-watch, or indulge in your latest hobby. If the thought of manually managing your money makes you want to take a long nap, you're in the right chapter. Welcome to the world of automation — where your financial growth cooks in the background, and you barely lift a finger.

Why Manual Money Management is So Last Season

Manual money management is like using a flip phone in the age of smartphones. Sure, it works, but why struggle when you can upgrade to something slicker, quicker, and smarter? Let's ditch the financial flip phone and automate our way to wealth.

Practical Strategy: Embracing the Financial Autobots

- **Direct Debit Delights:** First up, automate those bill payments. Late fees are the silent killers of good vibes and bank balances. Set up direct debits and never pay a late fee again.

- **Saving Without Thinking:** Next, let's automate your savings. Decide on a percentage of your paycheck that you won't miss (start small, think big) and set it to automatically transfer to a savings account. It's like playing financial hide and seek with future you as the winner.

Investing on Autopilot: Your Money's Personal Trainer

Think of automated investing as hiring a personal trainer for your wallet. It keeps your money fit, flexing, and growing without you having to sweat the details.

Practical Strategy: Effortless Investing

- **Robo-Advisors for the Win:** These digital financial planners are like having a Wall Street whiz in your pocket. They'll manage your investments, rebalance your portfolio, and you won't have to do a thing except check in now and then.

- **Recurring Investment Buys:** Set up a monthly buy-in for your favorite stocks, mutual funds, or ETFs. It's like a subscription box for financial growth—exciting to see what you'll accumulate over time.

Emergency Funds: Your Financial Safety Net

Building an emergency fund might not be glamorous, but it's essential. Automating this process is like building a financial safety net one knot at a time, without even realizing you're doing it.

Practical Strategy: The Stealthy Safety Net

- **Out of Sight, Out of Mind:** Set up a separate high-yield savings account for your emergency fund and automate contributions. Small, consistent transfers can build a significant buffer over time, and if it's out of your main banking sight, you're less tempted to dip into it.

The Beauty of 'Boring' Financial Success

Let's face it: the most effective financial strategies are often the most unexciting. Automating your finances may not give you the adrenaline rush of day trading or the thrill of timing the market, but it provides something far better — consistent, reliable growth without the stress or the guesswork.

Automating your finances is like setting up a slow cooker in the morning and coming home to a delicious meal — it does the work while you go about your day. By embracing automation, you're not just simplifying your financial life; you're supercharging it. So, go ahead, set it, forget it, and watch as your financial feast prepares itself. Welcome to the worry-free world of automated wealth accumulation.

There you have it, folks. The path to accumulating wealth needn't be paved with constant vigilance and manual labor. With automation as your ally, you're free to live your life, knowing your finances are not just in good hands — they're in your hands, working tirelessly in the background. Cheers to that!

The Debt Dilemma: Procrastination's Best Friend

Welcome to the Jungle, We've Got Fun and Games; and by "fun and games," I mean the kind of rollercoaster ride that makes you wish you'd stayed on the merry-go-round. Debt: it's the jungle gym of the financial playground, and if you're not careful, you'll find yourself stuck at the top, too scared to climb down. But fear not, intrepid explorer, because we're about to chop through the vines of debt with our trusty machete of wisdom and get you safely back on solid ground.

Why Debt Loves Procrastinators

Debt and procrastination go together like peanut butter and jelly, except this sandwich is the kind you find squished at the bottom of your bag, uneaten for weeks. The longer you ignore debt, the bigger and scarier it grows, until it's this monstrous blob shadowing your every financial move.

Practical Strategy: Face the Beast

- **Get Real with Your Debt:** Gather all your debt statements, yes, even the ones you've been using as coasters. Lay them out and tally them up. Knowing is half the battle.

- **The Snowball Method:** Start with your smallest debt. Pay it off. Then move to the next smallest. Each victory is a snowball getting bigger, rolling down the hill, gathering momentum.

Interest Rates: The Silent Debt Growers

Interest rates are like those sneaky weeds that grow twice as fast when you're not looking. One day, you owe a manageable amount; blink, and suddenly, it's like, "Where did all these zeros come from?"

Practical Strategy: Weed Whacking

- **Negotiate Lower Rates:** Call your creditors and charm them into lowering your rates. Okay, "charm" might be a stretch, but it doesn't hurt to ask.

- **Consolidate:** If you're juggling multiple debts with high-interest rates, consider consolidating them into one lower-interest loan. It's like herding cats into a basket so you can carry them with one hand.

Making Friends with a Budget

Budgeting is like that responsible friend who says, "Maybe we shouldn't have that fifth slice of pizza." It might be a buzzkill at the moment, but you'll thank them in the morning.

Practical Strategy: Befriending the B-Word

- **Track Your Spending:** For one month, write down everything you spend money on. Yes, even that candy bar. You'll be surprised where your money's going.

- **50/30/20 Rule:** Aim to spend 50% of your income on needs, 30% on wants, and 20% on savings and debt repayment. Adjust the percentages to fit your situation, but keep the structure.

The Power of Saying "No" (to Yourself)

Sometimes, the biggest obstacle between you and debt freedom is, well, you. Impulse buys, retail therapy, that sale you just can't miss — they all add up.

Practical Strategy: The 48-Hour Rule
Pause Before You Purchase: See something you "must" have? Wait 48 hours before buying it. Often, the urge to buy will pass, and you'll save yourself some cash (and some buyer's remorse).

Tackling debt isn't about depriving yourself of all life's pleasures; it's about making smarter choices that lead to a healthier financial future. By facing your debt head-on, negotiating smarter terms, embracing budgeting, and learning to control impulse spending, you'll find your way out of the jungle and into the clear, open space of financial freedom. So, grab that machete and let's start clearing a path — one smart decision at a time.

And there you have it, your no-nonsense guide to breaking up with debt. Remember, the journey might be tough, but you're tougher. Here's to conquering debt and reclaiming your financial peace of mind. After all, life's a playground, and you've got better things to do than hang around the debt jungle gym.

Savings: The Procrastinator's Paradox

If you've ever found yourself saying, "I'll start saving money... tomorrow," only to spend that savings on a late-night online shopping spree, then congratulations, you're human. Saving money is the financial equivalent of starting a diet on Monday; it always seems like a great idea until Monday actually rolls around. But fear not, fellow procrastinators, for there's hope yet. Let's turn that "I'll save tomorrow" into "I saved today, and it didn't even hurt."

Understanding the Savings Stalemate
The hardest part about saving isn't deciding to do it; it's actually doing it. Our brains are hardwired to seek immediate gratification — why save for a vacation next year when you can have that shiny new gadget now? It's

the classic battle between Future You and Present You, and too often, Present You has the upper hand.

Practical Strategy: Trick Yourself into Saving

- **Out of Sight, Out of Mind:** Automate your savings so a portion of your paycheck goes directly into a savings account. If you don't see it, you're less likely to spend it.

- **Name Your Savings Goals:** Instead of a generic savings account, create accounts for specific goals: "Dream Vacation," "Emergency Fund," or "New Car." It's harder to dip into an account when it has a name attached to your dreams.

Making Saving a No-Brainer

Let's be real; if saving requires too much thought or effort, we're not going to do it. The key is to make saving so easy, so ridiculously effortless, that even the king or queen of procrastination can't mess it up.

Practical Strategy: The Lazy Saver's Blueprint

- **Round-Up Savings Apps:** Use apps that round up your purchases to the nearest dollar and save the difference. Bought a coffee for $3.75? That extra $0.25 goes straight to savings. It's like finding change in the couch cushions, but digital.

- **The $5 Challenge:** Every time you get a $5 bill, save it. You'll be surprised how quickly they add up, and it turns saving money into a bit of a treasure hunt.

The Fine Art of Finding Extra Cash

One of the biggest myths about saving is that you need to have a lot of extra money to do it. Spoiler alert: you don't. You just need to know where to look.

Practical Strategy: Uncover Hidden Savings

- **Cut the Cord:** Still paying for cable plus five streaming services? Time to reassess. Dropping just one can add to your savings without cramping your style.

- **The Subscription Audit:** Take a hard look at your subscriptions and memberships. That gym membership you haven't used since last New Year's resolution? It's time to say goodbye.

Saving Without Feeling Deprived

Saving money doesn't mean you have to live like a hermit, forsaking all earthly pleasures. It's about finding a balance between enjoying the now and preparing for the future.

Practical Strategy: Savvy Spending

- **Budget for Fun:** Allocate a portion of your budget for "fun money." This way, you can indulge without guilt, knowing you're still meeting your savings goals.

- **Embrace Free Entertainment:** There's a world of free entertainment out there, from community events to nature hikes. Who says you have to spend money to have a good time?

Saving money as a procrastinator isn't about making monumental changes overnight. It's about setting yourself up for success with small, manageable tweaks that accumulate over time. By automating your savings, making it a game, and finding creative ways to enjoy life without breaking the bank, you'll see your savings grow without feeling like you're missing out. So here's to saving today — because why put off till tomorrow what you can start right now?

There you have it, the procrastinator's guide to saving money. Remember, every little bit counts, and with these tricks up your sleeve, you'll be on your way to financial security without having to overhaul your entire life. Cheers to smarter saving and living your best life, both now and in the future.

Turning Downtime into Dollar Time

The Art of Making Your Couch Profitable (No, Really)

So, you've spent another evening deep-diving into the abyss of your favorite TV series, emerging only for snacks and the occasional reality check. Sounds like a solid night, right? But what if I told you that couch could be your launchpad to financial freedom?

Why Side Hustles Beat Saying "I'll Start Tomorrow"

Let's face it, the idea of starting a side hustle is often met with as much enthusiasm as starting a diet. It sounds great in theory, but the couch is right there. Here's the twist: starting a side hustle doesn't mean giving up your sacred couch time. It means making that couch time work for you.

Practical Strategy: Match Your Hustle to Your Lifestyle

- **Passion Projects Pay Off:** Love knitting, graphic design, or writing? There are people out there willing to pay for that. Start small, maybe an Etsy shop for your crafts or freelancing on sites that match your skills with folks in need.

- **Leverage Your Laziness:** Yes, you read that right. Love binge-watching? Consider starting a blog or YouTube channel reviewing shows. Your couch time just became research.

Finding the Right Side Hustle for You

The perfect side hustle is the one that feels less like work and more like fun. If the thought of doing it makes you cringe, it's not the one for you. The trick is finding something that sparks joy, not dread.

Practical Strategy: The Side Hustle Swipe Right

- **List Your Loves and Loathes:** Start with what you enjoy and what you're good at. Then list what you absolutely can't stand doing. Somewhere in the middle is your side hustle sweet spot.

- **Trial and Error:** Don't be afraid to test out a few side hustles. Think of it as speed dating for your bank account. Some will be duds, but you're just one experiment away from finding "the one."

Time Management: The Side Hustler's Secret Weapon

One of the biggest myths about side hustles is that you don't have the time.

The truth? You do. It's just a matter of being smart about it.

Practical Strategy: The Power Hour

- **Find Your Power Hour:** Dedicate one hour a day to your side hustle. Just one. Whether it's an hour before work, during lunch, or instead of that TV show you've seen a hundred times, make it count.

- **Batch Tasks:** Group similar tasks together and tackle them in your power hour. Efficiency is your best friend here.

Turning Skills into Bills

Every skill you have, no matter how mundane it might seem, can be monetized. Yes, even that uncanny ability to name all the state capitals.

Practical Strategy: The Skill Audit

- **Make a List, Check It Twice:** Write down all your skills and hobbies, then hit up the internet to see who might pay for them. You'd be surprised at the niches out there just waiting for someone exactly like you.

- **Upskill for Upgrades:** Invest a little time in sharpening your skills or learning new ones. Online courses are plentiful, and many are free. Today's quirky hobby could be tomorrow's paycheck.

Your next financial breakthrough might just be sitting next to you on the couch, waiting for you to notice it. Side hustles are about making money in a way that adds value to your life, not stress. So, take that first step, however small. Who knew that turning your downtime into dollar time could be so rewarding? Here's to making your passions profitable, one side hustle at a time.

Remember, the goal of a side hustle isn't to replace your day job overnight (although that would be nice). It's about building something over time that brings you joy and extra cash. So, what are you waiting for? Dive into the side hustle game and watch your financial and personal satisfaction grow. Cheers to being productively lazy!

Financial Detox: Cleansing Your Cash Flow

The Great Financial Cleanse: Time to Purge the Excess

Ever feel like your finances are on a junk food diet? Overflowing with unnecessary expenses, late-night impulse buys, and a hefty dose of "where did all my money go?" syndrome? If so, welcome to your financial detox plan — a chance to cleanse your cash flow, flush out the fiscal toxins, and get your money's metabolism firing on all cylinders.

Why Your Wallet Needs a Detox

Just like our bodies crave a reset after too many cheat days, our finances occasionally need a purge of bad habits and unhealthy practices. This isn't about stripping down to financial bones but rather about removing the clutter that keeps you from seeing and reaching your money goals.

Practical Strategy: The Cash Cleanse

- **Spot the Spending Sappers:** For one week, track every penny that leaves your pocket. You're likely to spot a few financial vampires — recurring expenses that suck your budget dry without providing much in return.

- **Cut the Cord on Financial Drainers:** That gym membership gathering dust? Those subscription boxes filled with things you hardly use? Time for them to go. Think of it as decluttering your financial house.

Rehydrating Your Savings

A key component of any detox is hydration. In the world of finance, this means injecting liquidity back into your savings. It's about replenishing the well, ensuring you have a healthy reserve for both opportunities and emergencies.

Practical Strategy: Savings Infusion

- **Automate to Hydrate:** Set up an automatic transfer to your savings account right after payday. Treat it like a non-negotiable expense, similar to rent or utilities. You're paying Future You for services rendered.

- **The Spare Change Spa:** Utilize apps that round up your purchases and save the difference. It's a painless way to slowly but surely build up your savings, turning financial spare change into a therapeutic spa for your wallet.

Digesting Investments: Slow and Steady Wins the Race

Post-detox, it's vital to reintroduce elements back into your diet carefully. The same goes for investing. After clearing out the financial clutter, it's time to slowly and methodically introduce investments into your portfolio.

Practical Strategy: The Investment Diet

- **Start with the Basics:** Look into low-cost index funds or robo-advisors as a way to get your feet wet without diving headfirst into the deep end of complex investments.

- **A Taste Test Approach:** Dip your toes into various investment options in small amounts. It's like sampling a tasting menu — find out what suits your palate (risk tolerance) and stomach (investment goals) best.

Maintaining Financial Health Post-Detox

Detoxing is great, but maintaining that newfound financial clarity is where the real challenge lies. This phase is about building sustainable habits that keep your finances lean, mean, and clean.

Practical Strategy: The Daily Financial Smoothie

- **Morning Money Moments:** Spend five minutes each morning checking your accounts, reviewing your budget, and setting a financial intention for the day. It's the equivalent of a morning smoothie for your wallet — refreshing and nourishing.

- **Weekly Wealth Workouts:** Dedicate a bit of time each week to review your financial progress, adjust your budget as needed, and plan for upcoming expenses. Keeping your finances flexible and responsive ensures your detox wasn't in vain.

Embarking on a financial detox isn't about deprivation; it's about liberation. By cleansing your cash flow, hydrating your savings, and carefully curating your investment intake, you set the stage for a healthier, wealthier you. Remember, financial well-being isn't a destination; it's a continuous journey. With each mindful decision, you're not just detoxing your wallet; you're enriching your life.

And with that, you're equipped to embark on your financial detox journey, flushing out the bad habits and welcoming in a new era of fiscal fitness. Here's to a cleaner, leaner financial future that's not just about surviving but thriving. Cheers to your financial health!

Financial Independence: Breaking Up with Your Paycheck-to-Paycheck Lifestyle

The Ultimate "It's Not You, It's Me" to Your Paycheck-to-Paycheck Romance
Let's be real: Living paycheck to paycheck is like being in a bad relationship that you just can't seem to quit. It's comfortable, familiar, and oh-so-predictable, but deep down, you know you deserve better. So, how about we craft the perfect breakup text to that clingy paycheck-to-paycheck lifestyle? It's time to swipe right on financial independence and start a love affair with your bank account that's based on mutual respect (and interest).

Why You and Paycheck-to-Paycheck Aren't Meant to Be

Staying in this cycle is like eating fast food for every meal. Sure, it fills you up and it's easy, but it's not doing you any favors in the long run. Breaking free means more than just having extra cash; it's about taking control of your financial destiny.

Practical Strategy: The "We Need to Talk" Budget

- **Identify Your Non-Negotiables:** Start by figuring out what expenses are absolutely essential and which ones are more like that third coffee of the day – nice but not necessary.

- **The Breakup Budget:** Create a budget that prioritizes savings and debt repayment over impulsive buys. Think of it as choosing to stay in and binge-watch your favorite series instead of going out and blowing money you don't have.

Building a Financial Buffer: Your New BFF

One of the best ways to break up with the paycheck-to-paycheck cycle is to introduce a buffer between you and those awkward "end of the month" moments. This buffer isn't just a safety net; it's your ticket to financial peace of mind.

Practical Strategy: The Buffer Buddy System

- **Start Small, Think Big:** Begin by setting aside a small amount from each paycheck, gradually increasing it as you adjust your budget. Even a buffer of $100 can prevent a financial faceplant when unexpected expenses pop up.

- **Automate Your Savings:** Use automatic transfers to move money into your savings account as soon as you get paid. Out of sight, out of mind, and into your financial buffer.

The Side Hustle: Because Two Incomes Are Better Than One

Sometimes, breaking up with paycheck-to-paycheck means getting a little flirty with side hustles. In today's gig economy, finding a side gig that aligns with your interests and schedule is easier than ever.

Practical Strategy: The Side Hustle Swipe

- **Match Your Interests with Income:** Love pets? Try dog walking or pet sitting. Got a knack for crafts? Open an online shop. The perfect side hustle is

out there waiting for you to swipe
right.

- **Time Management Tango:**
  Balance is key. Make sure your
  side hustle doesn't interfere with
  your main source of income or
  personal well-being. It's a dance,
  not a sprint.

Investing in Yourself: The Ultimate Love Story

Investing in yourself might be the single most important step towards financial independence. This means education, skill-building, and personal development that opens doors to higher income opportunities.

Practical Strategy: The Self-Love Investment Plan

- **Learn to Earn:** Take advantage of free or low-cost online courses to boost your skills and your resume. The more you learn, the more you earn.

- **Network Like You Mean It:** Sometimes, it's not what you know but who you know. Attend industry meetups, join professional groups, and get your name out there.

Breaking up with a paycheck-to-paycheck lifestyle isn't about making drastic changes overnight. It's about small, deliberate choices that collectively steer you towards a future where financial worries are a distant memory. By creating a sensible budget, building a financial buffer, exploring side hustles, and investing in your personal growth, you're not just saying goodbye to financial stress — you're embracing a life of abundance and security.

So, here's to financial independence, the kind of relationship with money that's built to last, filled with mutual growth, respect, and yes, a bit of romance. Remember, the journey to financial freedom is a marathon, not a sprint. Pace yourself, celebrate your victories, and keep moving forward. Your future self will thank you.

Beyond the Book - Cultivating a Legacy of Financial Empowerment

Embracing Your Financial Evolution

As we close this chapter — both literally and metaphorically — on overcoming procrastination for financial gain, it's crucial to recognize that your journey doesn't end here. The pages of this book have equipped you with the tools, mindset, and strategies to break free from the chains of procrastination and step into a realm of financial empowerment. But what comes next?

The Continuous Journey of Financial Growth

Financial empowerment is not a destination but a continuous journey. As you venture beyond the confines of this book, remember that the principles of proactive planning, mindful spending, and strategic investing are not just chapters but chapters in the ongoing story of your life.

Practical Strategy: Cultivating Your Financial Garden

- **Plant Seeds for the Future:** Your actions today are the seeds for your financial future. Continue to invest in yourself, your knowledge, and your financial portfolio.

- **Tend to Your Financial Garden:** Regularly review and adjust your financial plan to adapt to life's inevitable changes. Like a garden, your finances require attention, nurturing, and sometimes a bit of pruning.

Building Your Financial Community

No one achieves greatness in isolation. As you've learned, building a financially savvy community can amplify your success. Seek out mentors, join financial literacy groups, and share your journey with others. By fostering a community of financial empowerment, you not only solidify your own foundation but also inspire those around you to embark on their journeys.

Leaving a Legacy

Ultimately, the knowledge and habits you've cultivated extend beyond your personal gain. They're a legacy you can pass on to family, friends, and even strangers who may find inspiration in your journey. Your transformation from procrastination to prosperity is a testament to the power of taking control of your financial destiny.

The final page of this book is merely the beginning of your adventure. Armed with the tools and insights you've gained, you're poised to write the next chapters of your financial story — one where procrastination no longer holds sway, and financial freedom is within your grasp. Go forth with confidence, curiosity, and a commitment to continuous growth. Here's to your financial empowerment and the endless possibilities that await.